The Palace of Holyroodhouse

OFFICIAL SOUVENIR GUIDE

NEMO ME IMPUNE LACESSIT

Contents

Introduction

The Palace of Holyroodhouse stands in a spectacular setting at the foot of the Royal Mile in Edinburgh, its walled gardens surrounded by open parkland. Holyroodhouse has been a royal residence for over 500 years, and while the Palace has not experienced the continuous royal occupation of Windsor Castle and Buckingham Palace, the other royal residences, it is closely associated with Scotland's turbulent past. Its unique and varied history reflects its differing, often intermittent, use by the monarchy over the centuries.

Holyrood is a house of many memories. Wars have been plotted, dancing has lasted deep into the night, murder has been done in its chamber.

Robert Louis Stevenson
Edinburgh, Picturesque Notes, 1878

Today the Palace is the official residence of Her Majesty The Queen in Scotland. The Queen is in residence at Holyroodhouse once a year, for a week during the summer, when she carries out a wide range of public engagements at the Palace, in Edinburgh and throughout Scotland. The State Apartments are also used frequently by

LEFT
HM The Queen accompanies Pope Benedict XVI as he receives flowers from local children at the entrance to the Palace during his four-day visit to the UK in September 2010.

RIGHT
The Palace front.

members of the Royal Family for events in support of the charitable organisations of which they are patrons.

This official souvenir guide provides an account of the history of the Palace, and a guide to the State Apartments and their use, and to the magnificent works of art on display.

FACTS AND FIGURES

Silver tea kettle and stand
from the Jubilee gift of
1935.

Sir David Wilkie
(1785–1841), *George IV*,
1829; in preparation for his
visit to Scotland, George IV
placed an order for a
complete Highland dress
outfit.

The Palace of Holyroodhouse stands overlooked by the dramatic Salisbury Crags and by Arthur's Seat, an extinct volcano dating back some 350 million years. Arthur's Seat is the highest peak of the range of hills occupying the 260 hectares of Holyrood Park, which was a royal hunting estate during the twelfth century.

♛ The longest and largest room in the Palace is the Great Gallery, which is decorated with 96 of the original 111 Jacob de Wet portraits of the real and legendary kings of Scotland, from Fergus I to James VII.

♛ Six plasterwork ceilings marked the

ceremonial route leading to the King's Bedchamber, in the Palace as it was rebuilt for Charles II. They were created by the English plasterers John Houlbert and George Dunsterfield.

♛ The silver banqueting service in the Royal Dining Room was designed for 100 guests and consists of over 3,000 pieces. It was presented to mark the Silver Jubilee of King George V and Queen Mary in 1935.

♛ The kilt and plaid in Royal Stewart tartan worn by George IV, in his portrait by Sir David Wilkie displayed in the Royal Dining Room, were made using 60 metres of satin, 30 metres of velvet and 16 metres of cashmere, and cost £1,354 in 1822.

♛ There are four hectares of formal garden, which play host to the annual Garden Party in July and create a striking contrast to the dramatic landscape of the 260-hectare Queen's Park which surrounds the garden.

Detail of the plasterwork ceiling in the Morning Drawing Room, originally Charles II's Privy Chamber; the corners are richly decorated with cherubs and eagles bearing the cipher of Charles II and the Honours of Scotland.

at the Palace during his State Visit in 2003, and in September 2010 The Queen received His Holiness Pope Benedict XVI at Holyroodhouse. Whenever The Queen is in residence the Royal Standard, rather than the Royal Banner of Scotland, is flown. His Royal Highness The Prince Charles, Duke of Rothesay, is resident for one week during the summer, carrying out official engagements.

The State Apartments are furnished with numerous fine paintings and other works of art, many of which have long associations with the palace. Treasures from the Royal Collection can also be seen in the changing exhibitions in The Queen's Gallery (see p. 26), opened in 2002 as part of The Queen's Golden Jubilee celebrations.

Holyroodhouse is a working royal palace and a centre for national life whenever members of the Royal Family are resident. The Queen holds investitures in the Great Gallery for the distribution of honours; audiences are held in the Morning Drawing Room; and a luncheon takes place in the Throne Room to celebrate the installation of new Knights to the Order of the Thistle, Scotland's oldest order of chivalry. The Queen and The Duke of Edinburgh also hold an annual Garden Party within the Palace grounds, to which Scots from all walks of life are invited. Occasionally the Palace is used for ceremonial visits by foreign heads of state. President Putin of Russia was entertained

HOLYROOD ABBEY

RIGHT

The symbol of Holyroodhouse is the stag's head with a cross between its antlers seen by David I in a vision when he was out hunting in the area.

BELOW

The east end of the nave, with the excavated and preserved remains of the transepts and choir in the foreground.

The origins of the Palace lie in the foundation of an Augustinian abbey in 1128 by David I (r.1124–53), on forested land below the slopes of Arthur's Seat, the old volcanic mound.

Legend attributes the founding to King David's vision of a stag with a cross or 'rood' between its antlers, similar to the legends associated with both St Eustace and St Hubert. The name Holyrood may also derive from the precious relic, supposedly a fragment of the True Cross, which had been brought to Scotland by David I's mother, St Margaret. The King dedicated his new religious foundation to the Holy Rood.

The simple first church was to prove too small for the requirements of the community and a new building programme was begun c.1195 and continued until c.1230, to provide a much larger and more ambitious structure. Extensive monastic buildings were added to accommodate the large community, including cloisters, a chapter house, a refectory and guest houses. The enlarged foundation prospered, and from an early date contained royal chambers for use by the sovereign.

By the time Edinburgh became the capital of Scotland in the fifteenth century, kings preferred to reside at the abbey, surrounded by pleasant gardens and a large park for hunting, rather than at Edinburgh Castle, on its exposed rocky summit. Many significant events took place within its precincts. James II (r.1437–60) was born at Holyrood in 1430, and was crowned, married and eventually buried in the abbey. James III (r.1460–88) married Margaret of Denmark there. Although the king and his retinue were initially housed in the abbey's guesthouse, by the second half of the fifteenth century they occupied specific royal lodgings. Eventually, these came to eclipse those of the abbey in both size and importance.

The abbey was completed c.1250, but the stone vault caused problems from an early date, and in the fifteenth century two levels of flying buttresses were added for support. The abbey suffered badly in the 1540s from destructive raids by English armies, and the nave is all that remains today of the abbey's original

BELOW

A page from the Holyrood Ordinal, a mid-fifteenth century liturgical manuscript written for use in Holyrood Abbey. An ordinal is a book of rules for the daily services throughout the year in an abbey or church.

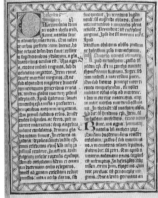

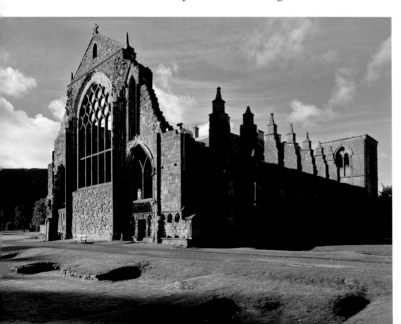

ABOVE
Looking down the nave of the thirteenth-century abbey.

THE ABBEY SANCTUARY

From the foundation of Holyrood Abbey, the precincts were a place of sanctuary, initially for all criminals, then, from the sixteenth century, for debtors only. The sanctuary area included the royal park and all inhabited houses within the abbey. Debtors, or 'abbey lairds' as they were known, were protected from the moment they crossed the sanctuary boundary, but were required to remain within on weekdays. On Sundays, when there could be no arrest, debtors could travel freely in the city, but had to return by midnight.

structure. The monastic buildings were abandoned after the Reformation and the abbey itself suffered from extensive damage. The nave was the only part retained for use and in 1633 underwent major renovation in preparation for the Scottish coronation of Charles I (r.1625–49). It was refitted for Catholic worship as the Chapel Royal during the reign of James VII and II (r.1685–88) and suffered further damage in 1688 when it was ransacked by an Edinburgh mob. In 1758 stone slabs were added to strengthen the roof of the building, but the extra weight hastened its collapse ten years later, leaving the abbey in ruins.

During the nineteenth century, the picturesque remains added to the romantic setting of the Palace. The scenic ruin attracted and inspired artists and writers: in 1829 the composer Felix Mendelssohn visited Edinburgh and was moved by the melancholy grandeur of the abbey to write his Scottish symphony.

In 1910–11, the site of the transepts and choir was excavated and the foundations left exposed in the garden, to allow the extent of the abbey church and its accompanying buildings to be visualised. In 2006 excavations by Channel 4's Time Team took place in the grounds as part of 'The Big Royal Dig'. These revealed walls and floors of some of the early monastic buildings.

ABOVE
Neil Oliver inspects a trench in the Palace gardens during Channel 4 Time Team's 'Big Royal Dig' in 2006.

The Occupants of the Palace of Holyroodhouse

JAMES IV AND JAMES V: THE FIRST PALACE

RIGHT
British school, *James V*,
*c.*1540.

BELOW
Thomas Sandby
(1721–98), *James IV's
gatehouse from the west*,
1746. Traces of this
building are still visible in
the north-west corner of
the present Forecourt; it
was built to serve both the
abbey and the Palace.

It was James IV (r.1488–1513), a frequent visitor, who decided to convert the royal lodgings in Holyrood Abbey into a palace. His impending marriage prompted him to commence building works to provide a suitable residence for his new bride, Margaret Tudor, daughter of Henry VII. The wedding was celebrated in the abbey church in August 1503. Although virtually nothing survives of the early palace buildings, it appears they were laid out around a quadrangle, occupying a similar position to the quadrangle of the present Palace, and a tower was added on the south side to provide extra accommodation for the sovereign. Excavations in 2006 revealed the outline of this building.

Further construction took place during the reign of James V (r.1513–42). Work began in 1528 on James V's Tower, a massive rectangular structure, rounded at the corners, intended to provide new royal lodgings at the north-west corner of James IV's palace. Designed in traditional Scottish style, the tower's prime function was residential, but it also provided a high degree of security; it was equipped with a drawbridge and probably protected by a

moat. This tower is the oldest part of the Palace that survives today.

The west front was rebuilt to house additional reception rooms. The elegant design incorporated a double-towered gateway, battlemented parapets, ornamental crestings, and large windows with great expanses of glazing. The south side was remodelled and included a new chapel; the old chapel became the Council Chamber. These domestic areas may have been begun in anticipation of James V's marriage in 1537 to Madeleine of Valois, daughter of Francis I, King of France. Madeleine died at the palace only 40 days after arriving in Scotland, but links with France were preserved by James's second marriage in 1538 to Mary of Guise, who was crowned in the abbey church.

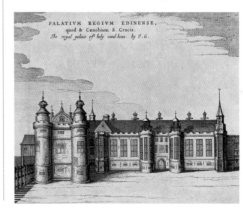

LEFT
Engraving of the west
front of the palace of
James V, by James
Gordon, *c.*1649.

OPPOSITE
James V's Tower today.

RIGHT

François Clouet (1510–72), *Mary, Queen of Scots in White Mourning*, c.1558–61. In this portrait, Mary is shown wearing white mourning to mark the loss of three members of her close family in a short time: her father-in-law, Henry II of France, died in 1559; her mother, Mary of Guise, in 1560; and her first husband, Francis II of France, later in the same year.

FAR RIGHT

Mary, Queen of Scots' Bedchamber, showing the door to the Supper Room in which Rizzio was attacked.

James V's daughter Mary (r.1542–67) succeeded to the throne of Scotland on her father's death in 1542, when she was only a few days old. During the 1540s, both the Palace and the abbey suffered badly from attacks by English troops during the Rough Wooing, when Henry VIII tried to force the Scots to accept a marriage between his son Prince Edward (the future Edward VI) and the infant Mary. In 1548 Mary was sent away to France to be brought up in safety at the French court, leaving Scotland in the care of her mother, Mary of Guise. Ten years later Mary married the Dauphin, the heir to the French throne. Following the sudden death of King Henry II of France in 1559, Mary's husband succeeded as Francis II, but he too died in 1560. The young Queen of Scots returned to Scotland in 1561, a Catholic in a strongly Protestant country. Mary came to live at Holyroodhouse, occupying the Queen's Apartments on the second floor of James V's Tower.

Many of the dramatic events of Mary's short reign took place in the abbey or Palace. She married her second husband, Henry Stuart, Lord Darnley, in the Palace chapel in 1565, and her Italian secretary, David Rizzio, was murdered by Darnley in her private apartments in

LEFT

Attributed to Hans Eworth (1520–after 1573), *Henry, Lord Darnley and his Brother Charles, 5th Earl of Lennox, c.*1562

ABOVE
British School, *Mary, Queen of Scots*, 1603–35.

left Scotland for England in 1568. Here, however, she was kept in captivity by Elizabeth I, who feared she would be a focus of Catholic conspiracies against the throne. Finally, in 1587, after the discovery of the Babington Plot against Elizabeth, she was executed at Fotheringay Castle.

LEFT
A plaque now marks the spot in Mary, Queen of Scots' Outer Chamber where Rizzio is believed to have died; above it hangs a seventeenth-century painting *Portrait of a man, known as 'David Rizzio'*.

THE MURDER OF DAVID RIZZIO

On the night of 9 March 1566 David Rizzio, Mary, Queen of Scots' Italian secretary, was brutally murdered in the Queen's Apartments at Holyroodhouse. The murderers were led by Henry, Lord Darnley, the Queen's second husband, who was violently jealous of Rizzio's influence over Mary. At the time, Mary was pregnant with their only child, the future James VI and I. Darnley led the conspirators up the narrow private staircase to the Queen's Bedchamber from his apartment on the floor below. He rushed in upon the Queen, her ladies and Rizzio, who were in the tiny Supper Room, off the Bedchamber. Despite clinging to the Queen's skirts, Rizzio was dragged to the adjoining Outer Chamber, stabbed 56 times and left to die.

1566. Mary then fled the Palace, giving birth to her son James a few months later at Edinburgh Castle. After Darnley's death in mysterious circumstances in 1567, Mary married her third husband, James Hepburn, Earl of Bothwell, in the Palace. The marriage was universally condemned and, after a confrontation with the Scottish nobility at Carberry Hill outside Edinburgh, Mary was imprisoned and forced to abdicate in favour of her infant son. She escaped and finally

THE OCCUPANTS OF THE PALACE OF HOLYROODHOUSE

RIGHT
Daniel Mytens
(c.1590–1647), *Charles I*,
1628; his Scottish
coronation took place
in the abbey nave.

Mary's son, James VI (r.1567–1625), took up residence in the Palace in 1579. Extensive repairs were carried out and the gardens were enlarged and improved. By the time his queen, Anne of Denmark, was crowned in the abbey in 1590, a large court was in residence and the household numbered around 600 people. From 1603, however, when James succeeded to the English throne as James I and the court moved to London, the importance of Holyroodhouse faded. Renovations had to be made prior to the King's return to Edinburgh in 1617.

The Palace and abbey were renovated further in 1633 for the Scottish coronation of James's son, Charles I (r.1625–49). Major repairs and additions were made to the surviving nave of the abbey, where the coronation was to take place. The solemn, anglicised service offended many Scots, however, and the King's ensuing religious inflexibility led to the signing of the National Covenant in Scotland in 1638 and the outbreak of the Civil War in 1639. Turmoil followed the execution of Charles I in 1649, and in 1650 the Lord Protector, Oliver Cromwell, travelled north to impose Parliament's authority on Scotland. After Cromwell's victory over the Scots at the battle of Dunbar, the Palace was occupied as a barracks by some of his troops and was damaged extensively by fire.

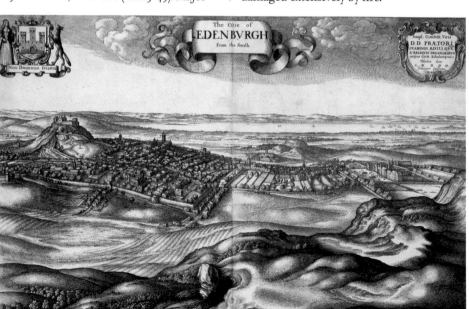

LEFT
Wenceslaus Hollar
(1607–77), *Bird's-eye
View of Edinburgh from
the South*, 1670, with
Holyroodhouse on
the right.

CHARLES II: THE REBUILDING OF THE PALACE

Charles II (r.1660–85) succeeded to the throne with the restoration of the monarchy in 1660. Holyroodhouse once again became a royal palace, and the regular meeting place of the Scottish Privy Council. A major rebuilding programme began in 1671 and the King took a close interest in the work, simplifying the plans to keep costs to a minimum. The designs were drawn up by the Scottish architect Sir William Bruce and the work was effectively overseen and directed by the Secretary of State for Scotland, John Maitland, Earl of Lauderdale (created 1st Duke of Lauderdale in 1672).

The successful design of the Palace as it is today is due to Bruce's skill in synthesising the new with the old, ensuring a smooth continuity with earlier buildings. The sixteenth-century north-west tower was balanced with a matching south-west tower, giving a symmetrical appearance to the new entrance façade. The towers were linked by a two-storey front, with a central entrance flanked by giant columns framing the Royal Arms of Scotland. Behind this screen, the existing quadrangular plan was retained and rooms were arranged around a courtyard with super-imposed classical pilasters. On the ground floor, the open, cloister-like

Quadrangle reflected the Palace's monastic origins. Bruce's classical design, combined with the sumptuous baroque interiors overseen by Lauderdale, placed Holyroodhouse in the forefront of fashion. The façades of the Quadrangle were the first wholehearted use of the classical orders in Scotland, and were to influence the design of numerous grand houses throughout the country.

By the end of 1674 the shells of the three main sides of the Palace and the new tower were virtually finished. Two years later the west front, which linked the towers, was completed.

The richly decorated interior of the Palace was created by the team of talented craftsmen brought to Scotland by the Duke of Lauderdale. The series of elaborate, high-relief ceilings, designed to emphasise the processional route, were by English plasterers John Houlbert and George Dunsterfield, who also

ABOVE
J.M. Wright (1617–94),
Sir William Bruce, 1664.

BELOW RIGHT
Sir Peter Lely (1618–80),
*Charles II, c.*1670.

LEFT
Bruce's classicising design for the Quadrangle introduced the Doric, Ionic and Corinthian orders to Scottish architecture.

15

THE OCCUPANTS OF THE PALACE OF HOLYROODHOUSE

worked for Lauderdale and Bruce in their private houses, Thirlestane Castle and Balcaskie. Alexander Eizat, a Dutchman, panelled the rooms in a classical style combined with ornate decorations. Fellow Dutchmen Jacob de Wet and Jan van Santvoort were responsible for the decorative painting and sculptural enrichment of the interiors. Both men worked on other Scottish country houses

LEFT
Sir Peter Lely, *The Duke and Duchess of Lauderdale*, c.1675.

BELOW
Roderick Chalmers, *The Incorporation of Wrights and Masons at Holyrood*, 1721, depicts the representatives of the various trades in front of the Palace.

A PROCESSIONAL ROUTE

A new State Apartment for the King was created on the east side, overlooking the planned Privy Garden, while accommodation for his queen, Catherine of Braganza, was formed from the old Royal Apartment in James V's Tower. A gallery running the length of the north side, now the Great Gallery, linked the King's and Queen's Apartments. Both sets of apartments included suites of rooms leading from a Guard Hall, through a Presence Chamber and a Privy Chamber, to an Ante-Chamber and a Bedchamber, the decoration progressively increasing in richness. As with the exterior, the classical orders were used in a hierarchy to denote the rising status of each room as the visitor approached the royal presence, following the example set by Charles II's cousin, the French king Louis XIV, at his palace of Versailles. The second-floor rooms were intended to provide space for the court when the King was in residence; for the remainder of the time they accommodated the officers of state or hereditary officers of the household.

ABOVE
A vista of aligned doors leads from the Morning Drawing Room to the Great Gallery on the east side of the Palace.

during this period, including Glamis Castle, the childhood home of Her Majesty Queen Elizabeth The Queen Mother. All these contributions created a striking baroque unity, particularly in the rooms that were completed at that time, such as the King's Bedchamber (see p. 40).

Finally, towards the end of Charles II's reign, de Wet was commissioned by the King to paint a sequence of 111 portraits of Scottish monarchs for the Great Gallery. These portraits not only preserved the likenesses of recent Stuarts, but also reasserted the Stuart succession to the throne.

Although Charles II and his queen never stayed at the newly rebuilt Holyroodhouse, his brother James, Duke of York and his wife, Mary of Modena, took up residence in 1679, and again in 1681–2. After his succession to the throne in 1685 as James VII of Scotland and II of England (r.1685–9), James had the Palace adapted for Catholic worship. In 1688, however, his Dutch Protestant son-in-law, William of Orange, landed in Devon to claim the throne on behalf of his wife Mary, James's older daughter. James was forced to flee to France. On hearing the news of William's arrival in London, a mob in Edinburgh ransacked the abbey and destroyed all traces of Catholicism.

The later Stuarts had little interest in their Scottish residence. The Palace was left in the care of the Duke of Hamilton, who had been appointed Hereditary Keeper. He took over the Queen's Apartments in James V's Tower and lived there in great luxury. Following the Act of Union in 1707, which united the kingdoms of Scotland and England, the Scottish Parliament was dissolved and the Council Chamber became redundant. Thereafter the Palace provided sumptuous grace-and-favour apartments for members of the Scottish nobility.

ABOVE
Sir Peter Lely, *James VII and II when Duke of York*, c.1665

BELOW RIGHT
The foundation inscription in the Quadrangle of the Palace; in abbreviated form it reads 'founded by Robert Mylne, Master Mason, July 1671'.

ABOVE
The plaster ceiling of the Grand Stair, the first in a carefully conceived progression along the processional route to the King's Bedchamber.

BONNIE PRINCE CHARLIE

Holyroodhouse briefly came to life once more as a royal palace when Prince Charles Edward Stuart (1720–88), known as Bonnie Prince Charlie, set up court at the Palace in 1745. The Catholic monarch James VII and II, Bonnie Prince Charlie's grandfather, was deposed in 1689, but continued to maintain his claim to the throne until his death in 1701. His son, James Francis Edward Stuart (1688–1766), the Old Pretender, led a failed attempt to regain the throne in 1715, and it was left to his grandson Bonnie Prince Charlie, the Young Pretender, to uphold the claim.

In 1745 Bonnie Prince Charlie launched an attempt to regain the crown for the Stuarts, landing on the west coast of Scotland and raising his father's standard at Glenfinnan. With support from the Jacobite clans of the Highlands, the Prince marched through Scotland with his army and seized Edinburgh. James VIII was proclaimed King of Scots, with his son as Regent. Four days later the Jacobites met a small British army at Prestonpans, just outside the city. The result was a resounding victory for Bonnie Prince Charlie's army and he returned to Edinburgh in triumph.

Bonnie Prince Charlie's entry into the Palace was recalled later by Lord Elcho, who had accompanied him: 'he mounted his horse and rode through St Anne's yards into Holyroodhouse amidst the cries of 60,000 people, who fill'd the air with their acclamations of joy'.

Holyroodhouse became the symbolic residence of the Stuart Prince in his Scottish capital; he conducted his official business in the Palace and lunched in public view. The Great Gallery became the setting for a ball

RIGHT
John Pettie (1834–93),
*Bonnie Prince Charlie
entering the Ballroom at
Holyroodhouse*, 1892.

in, broke and carried off all the fine gilded glasses, cabinets and everything else'. The destruction was not complete. In January 1746, after defeat by the Jacobites at Falkirk, the government troops billeted at the palace damaged de Wet's portraits of the Scottish kings. Before the decisive battle of Culloden, the Duke of Cumberland, commander of the Hanoverian troops and George II's son, also stayed in the Palace, occupying the same room that the Prince had so recently left.

In April 1746 Bonnie Prince Charlie and his Jacobite supporters were finally defeated by the Hanoverian army at Culloden. The Prince fled Scotland, spending his remaining years in Europe until his death in 1788.

'The Old Chapel Royal, or church of the convent, stands in its dishabille, ruined and decayed, and must fall down.'
Daniel Defoe, *A Tour Through the Whole Island of Great Britain* (1724–26)

and other evening entertainments, while during the day it possibly served as a guard chamber, as imagined in Sir Walter Scott's 1814 novel *Waverley*:

'A long, low, and ill-proportioned gallery, hung with pictures, affirmed to be the portraits of kings, who, if they ever flourished at all, lived several hundred years before the invention of painting in oil colours, served as a sort of guard chamber or vestibule to the apartments which the adventurous Charles Edward now occupied in the palace of his ancestors'.

Bonnie Prince Charlie left Edinburgh after six weeks, to march to England with his troops. Following his departure, soldiers from Edinburgh Castle, loyal to the Hanoverian king George II, arrived at the Palace, and in the words of a Jacobite lady, 'They have destroy'd the apartment the Prince was in, tore down the silk bed he lay

ROMANTIC RUINS

Little effort was made to maintain the Palace during the eighteenth century and the condition of its interior gradually deteriorated. The air of neglect which hung around the Palace encouraged its development as a tourist attraction, however, and the Romantic period, from the end of the eighteenth century, saw growing public fascination with Mary, Queen of Scots, her apartments, and the dramatic events that took place there.

David Roberts (1796–1864),
Ruins of the Abbey of Holyrood, 1823.

FRENCH ROYALTY

At the end of the eighteenth century Holyroodhouse provided a home for the comte d'Artois (1757–1836), the younger brother of Louis XVI of France, who had been in exile since the start of the French Revolution in 1789. He arrived in 1796, seeking refuge from large debts incurred on the Continent and taking advantage of the sanctuary offered by the abbey to debtors. He was accommodated in the faded splendours of the State Apartments, which had been neglected for many years but were substantially refurbished in advance of his arrival and during the following decade. Tapestries were cleaned, walls repaired and hung with canvas before being papered, carpets were laid and curtains made for windows and beds. Plain new mahogany furniture was provided by Edinburgh's leading furniture makers, Young, Trotter and Hamilton, similar to that supplied to the houses of Edinburgh's elegant New Town.

Artois, or 'Monsieur' as he was known, was joined at the Palace by members of his family and his servants, plus many of his faithful followers, forming a French colony in the city of Edinburgh. Artois remained at Holyroodhouse until 1803, although the rooms continued to be occupied by members of his suite until 1815. He eventually succeeded to the French throne as Charles X in 1824, but following the July Revolution in 1830 and his abdication, the exiled King once again took up residence at Holyroodhouse, accompanied by his young grandchildren. Furniture brought over from France was combined with the pieces previously used in his apartments. He finally departed two years later and remained in Europe until his death.

ABOVE
Engraving after C.A.d'Hardiviller of Henri, duc de Bordeaux, 1832. Charles X's grandson often wore Highland dress during his stay at Holyroodhouse.

LEFT
Sir Thomas Lawrence (1769–1830), *Charles X, King of France*, 1825 (detail).

BELOW
This dirk was part of the set of Highland accoutrements supplied to George IV in 1822. The blade is engraved with thistles and the badge of St Andrew.

A turning point in the history of the Palace as a royal residence came in 1822, when George IV (r.1820–30) visited Scotland, the first reigning monarch to do so since Charles I in 1633. The visit was encouraged by the Scottish writer Sir Walter Scott, who devised the King's programme and the accompanying pageantry. Although the King was lodged at the more comfortable Dalkeith Palace, Holyroodhouse was extensively tidied up and redecorated for the King to host a number of receptions.

A Great Drawing Room was created in Charles II's old Guard Chamber and hung with crimson cloth fringed with gold.

A contemporary account records, 'In compliment to the country, his Majesty appeared in complete Highland costume … which displayed his manly and graceful figure to great advantage' (see p. 6).

Before he left Edinburgh the King paid a private visit to his Palace and was shown around Mary, Queen of Scots' apartments by the Duke of Hamilton's housekeeper. The servants of the Duke of Hamilton ran a profitable sideline as tour guides, escorting visitors around James V's Tower, and describing in detail Rizzio's murder and the alleged bloodstain left on the floor. Many of the Duke of Hamilton's furnishings, which were deemed old-fashioned, had been moved from his apartments to Mary, Queen of Scots' rooms above, including the large, late-seventeenth-century State Bed (see p. 46; now in the King's Bedchamber), described by Sir Walter Scott as the 'couch of the Rose of Scotland'. George IV decreed that 'in repairing the palace, these apartments should be preserved, sacred from every alteration'. Following his visit, interest in the Palace increased; further improvements were made to the fabric of the building and some of the outlying buildings were removed.

ABOVE
Sir David Wilkie, *The Entrance of George IV at Holyroodhouse*, 1822–9. To his surprise, George IV received a rapturous welcome when he arrived in Edinburgh, and he entered the Palace as King of Scotland in a spectacular and symbolic ceremony. The first *levée*, or reception, was held at the Palace two days later, when he was introduced to 1,200 gentlemen, many of whom had queued for hours. He received guests in his Drawing Room or Throne Room, clad in full Highland dress, and later in the week held a reception at the Palace for over 400 ladies.

BELOW
S.D.Swarbreck, *Mary, Queen of Scots' Bedchamber*, 1861, showing the State Bed dominating the room.

QUEEN VICTORIA

Queen Victoria (r.1837–1901) first travelled to Scotland in 1842. This visit engendered a deep love of the country and led to the purchase of Balmoral Castle in Aberdeenshire as the Queen's Highland holiday home. She described Scotland as 'this most beautiful country which I am proud to call my own, where there was such devoted loyalty to the family of my ancestors.' Her love of Scotland resulted in a decisive change in the fortunes of Holyroodhouse, as the Palace was seen as a strategically placed stop on the long journey north to Balmoral. For the Scots, the Queen's return to the old Stuart palace was seen as an event of deep emotional significance, and Holyroodhouse was gradually reinstated as Scotland's foremost royal residence.

'We passed by Holyrood Chapel, which is old and full of interest, and Holyrood Palace, a royal-looking old place.'

Queen Victoria, *Journal*, 3 September 1842

The renovation of the dilapidated Palace was supervised from London in preparation for Queen Victoria's visit in 1850. Space was limited as there were still many grace-and-favour tenants, and it was the old State Apartments on the first floor that were restored for the Queen.

Robert Matheson, Principal Architect of

LEFT
George M. Greig (*fl*.1845–67), *The Presence Chamber or Evening Drawing Room*, 1863. This shows the *Africa* tapestry which Queen Victoria had brought up from Buckingham Palace, and which still hangs in the same room.

the Office of Works in Scotland, was determined that the quality and nature of the repairs should be worthy of the Palace's historical significance. He arranged for the redecoration to be carried out by David Ramsay Hay, Edinburgh's leading interior decorator. Hay cleaned the spectacular plasterwork ceilings in the State Apartments and repainted them in rich colours to complement the panelling and tapestries. Furniture left behind by previous tenants, together with that provided for the French Royal Family, was combined with pieces sent up from

Buckingham Palace.

Eventually, with the departure of most of the grace-and-favour tenants, the Queen and her family moved to apartments on the second floor, all decorated with the 'same pretty carpets and chintzes'. Queen Victoria was 'struck with the beauty of the edifice', and her frequent visits to Holyroodhouse turned the tide of neglect and ensured its future as a royal palace. It also brought the Palace to the centre of public attention and led to a demand for visits by an inquisitive public. Victoria paid her last visit to Holyroodhouse in 1886.

FORECOURT

Improvements were made to the immediate surroundings of the Palace, with Prince Albert, the Prince Consort (1819–61) taking a particular interest in these schemes. A magnificent fountain was installed on the Forecourt in 1859, as shown in this lithograph after J.H. Connop. It was modelled on the historic example at Linlithgow Palace to the west of Edinburgh.

RIGHT
David Jagger (1891–1958), *Portrait of Queen Mary*, 1929–30, commissioned to hang at Holyroodhouse.

FAR RIGHT
Frederick W. Elwell (1870–1958), *Portrait of King George V*. The King wears the mantle of the Order of the Thistle, 1932.

During the twentieth century Holyroodhouse became not only a regular royal residence and much-loved family home once more, but also an acclaimed visitor attraction. The Palace first came to life again in the reign of King George V (1910–36); in preparation for the first visit to Scotland in 1911 of the King and his consort Queen Mary, a number of renovations were carried out, including the installation of central heating and electric light, and repairs were made to the drainage system.

A further programme of improvements, including new bathrooms and modernised kitchens, was implemented after World War I, while the selection of Holyroodhouse as the site of the Scottish National Memorial to King Edward VII in 1922 provided an opportunity to enhance the external appearance of the Palace. The Forecourt was enclosed within richly decorated wrought-iron ornamental railings and gates and a statue of the King, by H.S. Gamley, was erected, facing the west front of the abbey.

ROYAL VISIT

King Edward VII (r.1901–10) made a brief visit to Holyroodhouse in 1903 while staying at Dalkeith Palace. He held *a levée* in the Throne Room and is shown here with a line of Scots before him, waiting to be presented. At the foot of the dais stands the Lord Chamberlain, and the Royal Company of Archers are on duty.

LEFT Messrs Dickinson, *The First Levée of Edward VII at the Palace of Holyroodhouse, 12 May 1903*.

OPENING THE PALACE TO VISITORS

From the mid-eighteenth century the apartments associated with Mary, Queen of Scots were shown to visitors by the Duke of Hamilton's housekeeper. In 1852, following Queen Victoria's visit, staff were appointed to show what became known as the Historical Apartments on a regular basis. Tickets cost sixpence during the week, but Saturday opening was free. Visitors were taken through the Great Gallery, the recently vacated first-floor apartments, which became known as the Darnley Rooms, and Mary, Queen of Scots' apartments. In 1925 the importance of Charles II's State Apartments was recognised and the public tour was extended to include these rooms.

The cost of these repairs led to a review of the Palace's role, and as a result, Holyroodhouse was recognised as the sovereign's official residence in Scotland. It began to be used on a regular basis for garden parties and ceremonies such as investitures and presentations.

King George VI (r.1936–52) and his consort Queen Elizabeth were regular visitors to Scotland. The daughter of the Earl of Strathmore, Queen Elizabeth had spent much of her childhood at Glamis Castle. The royal couple paid a first visit to Holyroodhouse in 1937 and then continued the tradition of regular visits, usually accompanied by their daughters, Princess Elizabeth and Princess Margaret.

Her Majesty The Queen paid her first official visit to the Palace shortly after her coronation in 1953. During the second half of the twentieth century the role of the Palace continued to expand and today, as the official residence of The Queen in Scotland, it is the focus of important state events as well as less formal visits by members of the Royal Family.

LEFT

The interior of The Queen's Gallery, showing the *Northern Renaissance* exhibition in 2011.

27

BELOW

The exhibition space on the first floor of The Queen's Gallery, during the *Canaletto in Venice* exhibition, 2006–07.

THE OCCUPANTS OF THE PALACE OF HOLYROODHOUSE

THE QUEEN'S GALLERY

In 2002 the new Queen's Gallery at Holyroodhouse was opened to celebrate The Queen's Golden Jubilee. Benjamin Tindall Architects of Edinburgh created the Gallery in the shell of the former Holyrood Free Church and Duchess of Gordon's School at the entrance to the Palace. The two buildings had been constructed in the 1840s with funds from the Duchess of Gordon, but fell into disuse in the late nineteenth century. The design of the Gallery complements the original nineteenth-century architecture, elements of which have been incorporated into the new spaces. The architect has also collaborated with a number of artists and specialist makers to create permanent and functional works both within and outside the Gallery.

The arched stone entrance, visible from the Royal Mile and directly opposite the new Scottish Parliament, unites the former school and church buildings and is presided over by Scotland's heraldic lion. The archway is decorated with a carved and gilded garland of Scottish flowers, including thistles and daisies. The gilded bronze hinges on the monumental oak entrance doors continue the heraldic and foliage themes. Inside, a decorated glass screen divides the reception area from the main exhibition space. A striking central stair of native timber leads, through a large archway, to the gallery spaces on the first floor, where the soaring ceiling incorporates the church's original roof trusses to dramatic effect.

The Gallery provides purpose-built, modern facilities for a rolling programme of exhibitions of works of art from the Royal Collection, to be shown in Edinburgh in tandem with exhibitions at The Queen's Gallery, Buckingham Palace.

Tour of the Palace

FORECOURT

The visitor approaches the Palace past The Queen's Gallery and through the restored and adapted Guardhouse, designed in a baronial style in 1861 by Robert Matheson. Beyond the Guardhouse lies the spacious Forecourt, with a large stone fountain at its centre, and enclosed by the wrought-iron gates and screens created by J. Starkie Gardiner as part of the Scottish National Memorial to Edward VII.

In July each year, at the start of The Queen's annual visit to the Palace, the Forecourt is transformed into a parade

ground for the Ceremony of the Keys, when the Lord Provost of Edinburgh presents The Queen with the keys to the City of Edinburgh.

LEFT
The Royal Regiment of Scotland provide a guard of honour for The Queen before the Ceremony of the Keys, 2011.

OPPOSITE
The entrance front was conceived as a triumphal gateway, surmounted by the Royal Arms of Scotland. Above, a crowned cupola with a clock rises behind a broken pediment supported by dolphins, on which are two reclining figures.

RIGHT
The Forecourt fountain and entrance to the Palace, winter 2010.

QUADRANGLE

The Palace, as rebuilt by Sir William Bruce in the reign of Charles II, is laid out round a central, classical-style Quadrangle, reached from the Forecourt through a triumphal entrance. Bruce deployed three of the five classical orders, Doric, Ionic and Corinthian in ascending order, on the façades of the Quadrangle, to emphasise the status of each floor. The overall effect is one of balance, symmetry and proportion. This represented a new style of architecture in Scotland, breaking completely with the tradition of fortified houses. The grand classical design was widely admired and copied throughout the country.

ABOVE
The Quadrangle, designed by Sir William Bruce, reflects the Palace's monastic origins with its cloister-like layout.

RIGHT
Thistle detail in the decorative stonework of the Palace.

GREAT STAIR

This imposing staircase, with its stone steps and balustrade, was designed by Sir William Bruce as the first stage in the processional route leading through the State Apartments to the King's Bedchamber on the first floor. The cantilevered stair, at the forefront of building technology at the time, and the spectacular plasterwork ceiling were intended to impress. The ceiling is the first in a series of six increasingly ornate plasterwork creations that originally decorated the rooms along the processional route. The decoration, built up on a timber framework, was created in moulds from plaster reinforced with horsehair, and applied and finished by hand. In the corners, figures of angels bear the attributes of kingship, the Honours of Scotland: the crown, the sceptre and the sword.

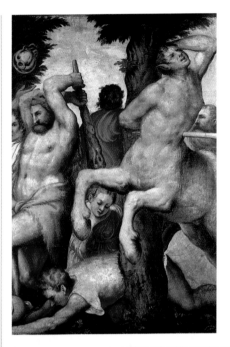

LEFT
Hanging on the walls of the Great Stair are eight detached and framed fresco fragments, c.1550, by the Italian artist Lattanzio Gambara (c.1530–74), showing scenes taken from Ovid's *Metamorphoses*. They were purchased by Prince Albert and have been displayed at Holyroodhouse since 1881.

BELOW
The Great Stair formed the first stage in the processional route that led to the King's Bedchamber.

ABOVE
Detail of plasterwork in the ceiling above the Great Stair, showing the lifesize figure of an angel holding the Scottish crown.

RIGHT
Louis-Gabriel Blanchet (1701–72), *Prince Charles Edward Stuart, the Young Pretender,* 1739; Bonnie Prince Charlie made the Palace the focus of his brief period of triumph in 1745, before his defeat by the forces of George II, and his portrait hangs in the Royal Dining Room

In Charles II's time this room was the Queen's Guard Chamber, at the start of the Queen's suite of rooms. Originally it would have been plainly finished, in keeping with this function. It was converted into an elegant neoclassical reception room around 1800, when it formed part of the apartments of the Duke of Hamilton. Although the decorative scheme is undocumented, the high quality of the plaster mouldings and the graceful screen of Ionic columns suggest the style of the Scottish architect Robert Adam. It was first used as a dining room at the end of Queen Victoria's reign, and it is still used as such today by The Queen and other members of the Royal Family.

JUBILEE GIFT OF SILVER

A silver banqueting service, designed for 100 guests, was presented by the Scottish benefactor Sir Alexander Grant to mark the Silver Jubilee of King George V and Queen Mary in 1935. The service, which comprises over 3,000 pieces, was commissioned specifically for use at Holyroodhouse. The design is based on Scottish examples of the early seventeenth century. It was made in Edinburgh by Henry Tatton and each piece is engraved with either the Scottish Coat of Arms or the Scottish Royal Crest. The service includes candelabra, tureens, salvers, plates, dishes, soufflé dishes, sauceboats, ladles, knives, forks, spoons, oyster forks, asparagus tongs, teapots, milk jugs and tea trays. The gift also included damask table linen; both the silver and the linen are still in use at the Palace today.

LEFT
Detail of the plasterwork cornice with an Ionic capital.

ABOVE
A pair of upholstered throne chairs, made for King George V and Queen Mary by Morris & Co. in 1911.

This was the King's Guard Chamber in Charles II's Palace, the first room of the elegant processional route which eventually led to the King's Bedchamber. The route was designed to ensure that access to the royal presence could be strictly controlled. Originally the Throne Room was plainly finished, with a simple cornice. It has been much altered subsequently, and its use has changed more than any other room in the Palace.

In 1822, for George IV's visit to Scotland, it became the King's Great Drawing Room, where he held *levées*, or receptions. It was hung with crimson cloth and the throne and canopy made for Queen Charlotte, the King's mother, was transported from Buckingham House.

A new plaster ceiling bearing the Royal Arms was installed for Queen Victoria in 1856, to give the room greater dignity. Until Queen Victoria managed to remove the grace-and-favour tenants from their apartments, this room was also used as her dining room. Queen Mary, however, described the ceiling as 'dreadful' and the room was altered again in 1929. A new ceiling was installed to reflect the character of the Charles II originals, and oak panelling, incorporating paintings, was applied to the walls.

STATE OCCASIONS

Today the Throne Room is used for receptions and other state occasions. In this room The Queen also holds a luncheon for the Knights and Ladies of the Order of the Thistle, on the occasion of the installation of a new Knight.

LEFT
The Duke and Duchess of Rothesay, as the Prince of Wales and the Duchess of Cornwall are known in Scotland, attend a reception in the Throne Room in 2008.

LEFT
The Evening Drawing Room, showing the *Africa* tapestry from *The Four Continents* series hanging on the far wall.

BELOW
Detail of *Asia*, from *The Four Continents* series, workshop of Peter and Franz van der Borght, Brussels, *c*.1750.

EVENING DRAWING ROOM

This room was the Presence Chamber of Charles II's Palace, where important visitors would have been received by the King. The ornate plasterwork ceiling is one of the original series designed to mark the processional route to the King's Bedchamber.

Queen Victoria arranged for the four tapestries hanging here to be sent up from Buckingham Palace in 1851, to give the room an air of richness and warmth. During her residence the room was used by the court as a drawing room. Today The Queen and the other members of the Royal Family use it for receptions.

THE TAPESTRIES OF HOLYROODHOUSE

In the sixteenth and seventeenth centuries, tapestries were the main decorative component of royal palaces, but they were displayed only when the monarch was in residence. Although 13 sets of tapestries were recorded at Holyroodhouse when Mary, Queen of Scots arrived in 1561, none of these survive at the Palace. An inventory compiled after the death of Charles II in 1685 recorded two sets of tapestries which are still hanging at the Palace: the *History of Diana* and the *Destruction of Troy*. Tapestries noted as hanging in the apartments of the grace-and-favour residents by 1700 and which remain in the Palace today include two Brussels panels of *Alexander the Great* and the four panels of the *Story of Tobit*.

ABOVE
Detail of English (Mortlake) *Diogenes* tapestry, 1682–3, originally bought for Charles II, and sent to the Palace on the instructions of Queen Victoria.

Many more tapestries were brought to Holyroodhouse in the nineteenth century. Queen Victoria took a lively interest in furnishing the Palace, as she and her growing family stayed there regularly on their way to and from Balmoral. In 1851 the eighteenth-century tapestries of *Africa* and *Asia* were brought up from Buckingham Palace and four late sixteenth-century panels of *The Planets* were dispatched from Hampton Court. A number of others were sent to Holyroodhouse in 1882, on the instruction of Queen Victoria. These included the Mortlake *Diogenes* panels, which had originally been purchased for Charles II in 1683.

The tapestry collection is an integral part of the history of the Palace and there is now an active programme of care and conservation of this historic collection.

RIGHT
French (Paris) tapestry of the *Death of Orion* (detail) from the *History of Diana* series, *c*.1630. This hangs in the King's Ante-Chamber.

ABOVE
Tapestry conservation work in progress.

MORNING DRAWING ROOM

BELOW
Plasterwork heraldic
unicorn springing from
a delicately modelled
rosebud on the long
central ceiling panel.

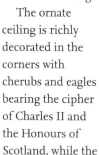

BELOW
Plasterwork heraldic
unicorn springing from
a delicately modelled
rosebud on the long
central ceiling panel.

This sumptuously decorated room was originally Charles II's Privy Chamber. The rich interior indicates the exclusive use of the room, where only privileged visitors would have been allowed more private access to the King.

The ornate ceiling is richly decorated in the corners with cherubs and eagles bearing the cipher of Charles II and the Honours of Scotland, while the long central panels feature heraldic lions and unicorns. The seventeenth-century panelling incorporates in the overmantel elaborate foliate carvings by the Dutchman Jan van Santvoort, which enclose a painting by his compatriot, Jacob de Wet, the first in a series of overmantel paintings in the Palace by this artist, who also painted the royal portraits in the Great Gallery.

The room was extensively renovated in 1850 for Queen Victoria, when the Edinburgh decorator D.R. Hay painted the ceiling in rich colours to complement the seventeenth-century tapestries. Queen Victoria used the room as her private drawing room; at that time, Jacob de Wet's painting was thought unsuitable and was covered with mirror glass. During the renovations carried out for King George V and Queen Mary, the colourful ceiling was painted out in white.

LEFT
The Morning Drawing Room; its walls are hung with French tapestries illustrating the story of the hunting goddess Diana, which were purchased for Charles II in 1668. They have been hanging here since at least 1796, when this was one of several rooms used by the comte d'Artois, the future Charles X of France.

RIGHT

Mahogany settee in the Morning Drawing Room, covered with silk and wool embroidery, upholstered by John Schaw of Edinburgh, c.1740.

BELOW

Mahogany side chair covered with silk and wool embroidery, mid-eighteenth century, one of a set in the Morning Drawing Room.

PRIVATE AUDIENCES

Today The Queen uses the room to give private audiences, for example to receive the First Minister of Scotland, the Lord High Commissioner and other visiting dignitaries.

LEFT

The Queen presents the late Donald Dewar with the Royal Warrant of Appointment, confirming him as the inaugural First Minister in the newly devolved Scottish Parliament, July 1999.

ABOVE

The Queen gives a private audience to Scotland's First Minister, Alex Salmond, in 2010.

KING'S BEDCHAMBER

ABOVE
The King's Bedchamber,
the most lavishly
decorated of the State
Apartments.

KING'S ANTE-CHAMBER

The decoration of this room is more
restrained, to suit its smaller scale and
function; it was originally a waiting room
for the King's Bedchamber beyond, and
also has impressive views over the garden.
In 1850 it served as Queen Victoria's
bedroom, and furniture for her use was
brought from Buckingham Palace and
Windsor Castle.

Designed as Charles II's Bedchamber,
this room is the culmination of the
processional route through the Palace. Its
great importance is emphasised by the
room's position on the central axis of the
building, like Louis XIV's bedchamber at the
French royal palace of Versailles. The lavish
decoration reinforces its significance; the
room contains the finest plasterwork,
decorative painting and carving in the
Palace. It was intended to be seen by only
the most privileged visitors.

The ceiling is the only one in the Palace
to have been completed with a central
decorative panel, painted by Jacob de Wet

in 1673 and showing *Hercules Admitted to Olympus*. This panel is enclosed by elaborate decorative plasterwork, which includes the crowned Thistle of Scotland. The overmantel painting, also by de Wet, continues a further flattering comparison of Charles II with Hercules, where the infant hero is seen strangling one of the serpents sent to kill him. The rich carved surround of the overmantel and the lions framing the marble chimneypiece are as elaborate as the ceiling decoration.

The principal focus of the room is now the State Bed (see p. 46), recorded in the Duke of Hamilton's apartments at Holyroodhouse from 1684. In 1976 the bed was restored and rehung with red damask to match the original fabric.

KING'S CLOSET

Designed as the King's Study, the private character of the Closet is reflected in its small size. The coved ceiling incorporates the Royal Coat of Arms, paired with fantastic cartouches of Charles II's cipher, and the spandrels are decorated with military trophies, a theme echoed in the carvings of antique armour framing the overmantel. Jacob de Wet's painting depicts *The Finding of Moses*, emphasising the legendary antiquity of the royal house of Scotland by alluding to its mythical descent from Pharaoh's daughter Scota. The panelled walls are hung closely with tapestries, in the seventeenth-century manner. In 1850 this room became Queen Victoria's breakfast room and was hung with green and gold flock wallpaper.

RIGHT
Detail of the carved lion's head on the fireplace surround in the King's Bedchamber.

LEFT
Detail of the overmantel carving in the King's Closet.

RIGHT
The Great Gallery, the largest room in the palace, is often used for investitures, dinners and receptions.

The largest room in the Palace, the Great Gallery connects the King's Apartments on the east side with the Queen's Apartments in James V's Tower to the west. Sir William Bruce devised a simple classical scheme for the room, which features a pair of black marble chimneypieces within Doric surrounds, framed by Ionic pilasters. The most notable decorative feature of the room is the extensive series of portraits, hung on every wall, of real and legendary kings of Scotland, supplied by Jacob de Wet between 1684 and 1686.

The Great Gallery has served many purposes over the years. After the Union of Parliaments in 1707 it was used for the election of delegates from among Scotland's peers to attend Parliament in Westminster. In 1745, during the Jacobite occupation of Edinburgh, Bonnie Prince Charlie held a ball in this room, and only a few months later, government forces were quartered here. While the comte d'Artois was in residence, a Catholic chapel was established in the Great Gallery.

Early in the twentieth century, King George V improved the service arrangements and had lifts installed between the ground floor, where the kitchens are located, and the first floor, in order for the Gallery to be used as the State Dining Room.

Today the Great Gallery is used regularly by The Queen to carry out investitures for Scottish recipients of honours. It is also used for state banquets, dinners and receptions.

RIGHT
The Great Gallery, the largest room in the palace, is often used for investitures, dinners and receptions.

TAM O'SHANTER CHAIR

This oak chair is closely associated with the great Scottish poet Robert Burns. The back of the chair is decorated with brass plaques on which are engraved the lines of Burns' poem, *Tam O'Shanter*. The chair is made from the timbers of the kirk at Alloway, Burns' birthplace; when the roof of the church collapsed at the end of the eighteenth century, its timbers were reused to make items associated with Burns. The chair was acquired by George IV in 1822, the year of his visit to Scotland.

ABOVE
This elaborately decorated bog oak chair, made in 1850 from ancient wood found in the peat marshes of Ireland, is carved from a single, unusually large, piece of bog oak.

The Dutch painter Jacob de Wet (c.1640–97) was commissioned by Charles II to paint the portraits of 110 kings of Scotland for the Great Gallery. Illustrating both real and legendary kings, from Fergus I in 330BC to Charles II, the series was essentially a political statement to promote the long line of the Stuart dynasty in the newly built Royal Palace.

Jacob de Wet, who came to Scotland in 1673, was initially employed by the architect Sir William Bruce to paint a series of overmantels in the Palace. The final contract for the kings of Scotland commission was signed in 1684, when de Wet agreed to spend two years on the paintings for a payment of £120 per year. Due to the death of Charles II before the completion of the job, de Wet was asked to paint an additional portrait of the new King, James VII, for the sum of £30.

The only Stuart to use the Gallery for its intended purposes was Bonnie Prince Charlie in 1745, when he held a ball surrounded by the portraits of his ancestors. After Bonnie Prince Charlie's victory at the battle of Falkirk in January 1746, the defeated government troops were billeted at the Palace. An anonymous journal records that the troops 'exercised the fury of their swords upon the fine pictures of many of the kings of Scotland for the defeat they received at Falkirk from their lineal descendants'.

The portraits were repaired and by 1826, 'after having been moved from their hanging frames, fixed in the panels of the wainscoting', although a number still hung loose in the window embrasures at the end of the nineteenth century. A further programme of cleaning and restoration was completed in 2003.

RIGHT
Jacob de Wet, *Fergus I*, *fl.c.*330BC, legendary founder of Scotland.

CENTRE RIGHT
Jacob de Wet, *Macbeth* (1005–47), King of Scots 1040–57.

FAR RIGHT
Jacob de Wet, *Robert the Bruce*, (1274–1329), King of Scots 1300–29.

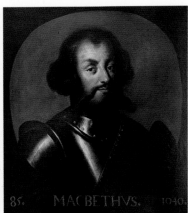

QUEEN'S LOBBY

This is the first of the rooms which formed the old Royal Apartments in James V's Tower, and which were refitted in 1671 for Catherine of Braganza, Charles II's queen, but never inhabited by her. Architect Sir William Bruce imposed order on this old, irregular room. The character of this and the following rooms remains simple, however, especially in contrast with the baroque splendour of the King's Apartments. There is a display relating to the Order of the Thistle in this room.

ORDER OF THE THISTLE

The Most Ancient and Most Noble Order of the Thistle is the highest order of chivalry in Scotland. It was James VII and II who firmly established the Order in 1687, to reward Scottish peers who supported the king. The number of Knights was limited to 12. George IV wore the insignia of the Thistle during his visit to Scotland in 1822; following this, a statute established the complement of Knights at 16.

The Queen is Sovereign of the Order and personally appoints Knights Brethren of the Thistle. The Order honours distinguished Scottish men and (from 1987) women who have contributed in a particular way to national life. The number of Knights remains at 16, together with three Royal Knights.

The insignia of the Order consists of a collar, badge and star. The motto is *Nemo me impune lacessit*, meaning 'no-one provokes me with impunity'. The patron saint of the Order is St Andrew, who appears on the badge.

ABOVE
The diamond-set Thistle Star, *c.*1820.

QUEEN'S ANTE-CHAMBER

During the 1560s this room and the Queen's Bedchamber were used by Lord Darnley, second husband of Mary, Queen of Scots. Following the rebuilding of the Palace by Sir William Bruce, they became part of the Queen's Apartments. This room was remodelled by Bruce after 1671, but the great thickness of the walls is still evident, revealing the ancient defensive origins of this part of the Palace.

The Duke of Hamilton took over the rooms in James V's Tower from 1684, and by the early eighteenth century this room was the Duke's dining room, furnished with elegant Georgian furniture. Any outmoded furniture, particularly that from the baroque period, was moved upstairs to the apartments formerly occupied by Mary, Queen of Scots. There they were included in the guided tours conducted by the Duke of Hamilton's servants. In due course the Duke also allowed visitors to view the first-floor rooms as part of their tour, and these became known as the Darnley Rooms.

When responsibility for opening the historical apartments to visitors passed to the Commissioners of Works in 1854, the rooms were redecorated and the panelling was grained 'in imitation of old oak'. Additional furniture and tapestries were acquired, and many of these pieces remain on display in this room.

BELOW

The Queen's Ante-chamber, showing two of the four English (Mortlake) *Playing Boys* tapestry panels, first half of the seventeenth century.

QUEEN'S BEDCHAMBER

Originally this room was the King's Bedroom. When it became part of the Queen's Apartments in the 1670s it was probably the Queen's Dressing Room and was remodelled by Bruce. The bed on display in this room (see p. 46) was originally supplied to the Duke of Hamilton in 1682, and was moved here from the second floor in the early twentieth century.

TURKEY-WORK CHAIRS

An extensive consignment of chairs was purchased in the 1660s to furnish the meeting rooms of the Privy Council at Holyroodhouse. The chairs were upholstered with Turkey work (detail below), a type of seat and backrest covering with a knotted woollen pile and colourful designs of stylised flowers on a dark background, in imitation of Turkish carpets.

THE STATE BED

This was not originally the king's bed, but was made for the Duke of Hamilton, the Hereditary Keeper of the Palace, and was part of the furnishings of his grace-and-favour apartment from 1684 until 1740, when a new bed was ordered. The bed was moved to Mary, Queen of Scots' Bedchamber, where, in its tattered state, it was described as Queen Mary's bed.

Many nineteenth-century depictions of this room show the bed in place (see illustration on p. 21).

The bed underwent extensive conservation in 1976. The original red damask survives on the headboard, the cornice and the canopy. The curtains and bedcover, which had disintegrated in the nineteenth century, were replaced.

BELOW
The State Bed: detail of the canopy.

THE 'DARNLEY' BED

This richly decorated tester bed, with a canopy covered with crimson and gold velvet and festoons of silk fringe, surmounted by four velvet-covered vases topped with ostrich feathers, was supplied to the Duke of Hamilton in 1682, by the London upholsterer John Ridge, for £218.10.

In 1745, Bonnie Prince Charlie occupied the Duke of Hamilton's apartments and slept in this bed. Shortly afterwards it was used by his adversary, the Duke of Cumberland. During the later eighteenth century, when the Hamiltons acquired more fashionable furniture, this bed was moved to Mary, Queen of Scots' Outer Chamber, where it was described by guides as Charles I's bed. The red damask State Bed, now on display in the King's Bedchamber, was in the adjacent

room and was described as Mary, Queen of Scots' bed. During the 1860s, when Lord Darnley's apartments on the floor below were renovated, the bed was moved down and became known as Lord Darnley's bed.

The bed has undergone conservation, and is placed behind glass with reduced light levels to protect the fragile textiles. The bedcover, applied with chinoiserie embroidery in silk and metal thread, was probably made in England around 1700. It was presented to Edward VII in 1910, and at that time was believed to have belonged to Henry VIII and his second wife, Anne Boleyn.

LEFT
The Darnley Bed: detail of the embroidered bedcover, *c.*1700

MARY, QUEEN OF SCOTS' CHAMBERS: BEDCHAMBER AND SUPPER ROOM

The rooms on the second floor of James V's Tower were occupied by James V's daughter, Mary, Queen of Scots, from 1561 until 1567. It was here, in the Queen's private apartments, that the brutal murder of Mary's secretary David Rizzio took place (see p. 13). The association of these rooms at Holyroodhouse with Mary's turbulent reign and this dramatic event has fascinated and thrilled visitors since the eighteenth century.

A small spiral staircase leads from what is now the Queen's Bedchamber up to Mary, Queen of Scots' Bedchamber. The Queen's tiny Supper Room is in the turret just off the Bedchamber and it was here that the Queen, her ladies and her secretary David Rizzio were dining on the night that Rizzio was murdered.

The Bedchamber has a compartmented oak ceiling, probably dating from the mid-sixteenth century. The initials *IR* and *MR* on the panels are those of James V and his Queen, Mary of Guise, the parents of Mary, Queen of Scots. Below the ceiling is a deep frieze, painted in grisaille with the Honours of Scotland, arabesques and cornucopia to mark Mary's arrival at the Palace.

When the Palace was remodelled by Bruce in the 1670s, the Queen's Apartments were relocated to the floor below and the second-floor rooms fell into disuse. They were later appropriated by the Duke of Hamilton.

LEFT

This seventeenth-century Flemish cabinet, veneered in red tortoiseshell with silver and silver-gilt mounts and on a nineteenth-century stand, is inscribed as having belonged to Mary, Queen of Scots and stands in her Bedchamber.

LEFT
Mary, Queen of Scots'
Bedchamber.

BELOW
Looking from Mary,
Queen of Scots'
Bedchamber into the
Supper Room where she
and her ladies were dining
with Rizzio on the night of
his murder.

THE PRESENTATION OF MARY, QUEEN OF SCOTS' CHAMBERS

By the mid-eighteenth century, the attention of visitors to the Palace focused on the rooms of Mary, Queen of Scots. Their gloomy spiral staircases, thick walls and heraldic ceilings, combined with details of Mary's tragic life and the story of Rizzio's murder, exerted a powerful appeal. Many of the Duke of Hamilton's unwanted items of furniture had been placed in the second-floor rooms and these pieces gradually came to be passed off to visitors as Mary, Queen of Scots' own possessions.

As early as 1760 the future Duchess of Northumberland recorded in her diary: 'I went also to see Mary Queen of Scots' Bedchamber (a very small one it is) from whence David Rizzio was drag'd out and stab'd in the ante room where is some of his Blood which they can't get wash'd out.'

Both George IV and Queen Victoria wanted to preserve these apartments with little change, but by the early twentieth century this began to look like neglect. Scholarship had improved and visitors began to question the authenticity of what they were shown. Through a succession of repairs much of the romantic visual appeal was lost, and in the mid-1970s the decision was taken to strip the rooms back to their essentials and to move the baroque furnishings to the King's Apartments on the first floor. Mary, Queen of Scots' chambers have now been re-presented to enhance the powerful and romantic mood for which they have long been famous.

LEFT
Queen Mary's Bedchamber, 1862–3, lithograph after George M. Greig (*fl.*1845–67); the State Bed, now on display in the King's Bedchamber, can be clearly seen.

BELOW
Lieven de Vogeleer (*fl*.1551–68), *The Memorial to Lord Darnley*, *c*.1567. This painting was commissioned by the bereaved parents of Mary's second husband, Lord Darnley, and depicts his family and infant son, James VI, mourning Darnley as he lies on his tomb.

51

TOUR OF THE PALACE

MARY, QUEEN OF SCOTS' OUTER CHAMBER

This is the room where Mary received visitors and where her formidable encounters took place with the intractable Protestant reformer, the cleric John Knox, who had preached against the Catholic Mary and condemned her for hearing mass, dancing, and wearing elaborate clothes. It is also the room in which Rizzio was stabbed and his alleged bloodstain can be seen in the place where his body was left.

At the east end of the room is Mary's oratory. The ceiling panel of the small oratory recess is decorated with the Cross of St Andrew encircled by a royal crown. In Mary, Queen of Scots' time, a window in this recess looked directly down on the west entrance of Holyrood Abbey. The stained glass window by Louis Davis, showing David I's mother St Margaret, dates from 1927.

LEFT
Mary, Queen of Scots' oratory.

The Outer Chamber is now devoted to a display of Stuart and Jacobite relics collected by or presented to successive sovereigns. The collection consists of treasures associated with Mary, including the Darnley Jewel, as well as relics of the later Stuarts, such as the silver-gilt caddinet (personal dining tray) made in Rome for Cardinal York, the brother of Bonnie Prince Charlie.

Many pieces were acquired by Queen Mary, consort of King George V, who took a great interest in objects of family history, sorting and classifying them by type. The Stuart Collection was moved to Holyroodhouse from Windsor Castle in 1995 and is now displayed in cabinets designed by Alec Cobbe, which draw on the early seventeenth-century Scottish fashion for extravagant funerary monuments.

LEFT
One of the cabinets specially designed to house the Stuart Collection.

BELOW
Nicholas Hilliard (1547–1619), *Mary, Queen of Scots*, miniature, 1574–6.

EMBROIDERY BY MARY, QUEEN OF SCOTS

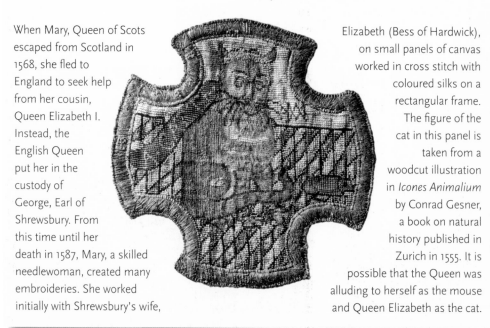

When Mary, Queen of Scots escaped from Scotland in 1568, she fled to England to seek help from her cousin, Queen Elizabeth I. Instead, the English Queen put her in the custody of George, Earl of Shrewsbury. From this time until her death in 1587, Mary, a skilled needlewoman, created many embroideries. She worked initially with Shrewsbury's wife, Elizabeth (Bess of Hardwick), on small panels of canvas worked in cross stitch with coloured silks on a rectangular frame. The figure of the cat in this panel is taken from a woodcut illustration in *Icones Animalium* by Conrad Gesner, a book on natural history published in Zurich in 1555. It is possible that the Queen was alluding to herself as the mouse and Queen Elizabeth as the cat.

RIGHT
Silver-gilt caddinet made in Rome for Bonnie Prince Charlie's brother, Prince Henry Benedict Stuart, Cardinal York.

LEFT
Pomander, c.1550, believed to have been used by Mary, Queen of Scots.

THE DARNLEY JEWEL

This spectacular jewel, intended to be worn at the neck or on the breast, was probably made for Lady Margaret Douglas, Countess of Lennox (1515–78), following the death of her husband, Matthew, Earl of Lennox, Regent of Scotland, in 1571. Margaret, the mother of Lord Darnley, was the granddaughter of Henry VII of England and first cousin of Queen Elizabeth I.

The heart-shaped jewel is made from coloured enamels, rubies, blue glass and an emerald. It is elaborately decorated on the cover, the reverse and the interior with many emblems and inscriptions, while compartments conceal further emblematic devices. These allude to the turbulent history of the Lennox family and probably also refer to Lady Margaret's hopes and ambitions for her grandson, James, son of Mary and Lord Darnley, who later became James VI and I.

The jewel was purchased by Queen Victoria in 1842 from the collection of the antiquarian Horace Walpole.

ABOVE
Letter from Mary, Queen of Scots to Charles IX of France, 1560–74, younger brother of her first husband Francis II.

GARDENS

ABOVE
'Queen Mary's Sundial'.

The four-hectare Palace gardens are encircled by the Queen's Park and form a contrasting foreground to the spectacular natural landscape beyond.

Until the time of James IV the gardens were primarily under monastic control. By the time Mary, Queen of Scots was resident at the Palace there was a series of enclosed gardens, including a walled Privy Garden to the north, and areas for cultivation and recreation. Jousting and archery took place within the grounds and there was a tennis court to the west of the Palace. Further works were undertaken at the time of James VI's visit in 1617 and for Charles I's Scottish coronation in 1633.

The two surviving relics of this early garden are 'Queen Mary's Bath', probably a sixteenth-century garden building to the north-west, and 'Queen Mary's Sundial', a multi-faceted sundial designed and carved by John Mylne in 1633, which can now be seen in the North Garden.

During the 1670s a Privy Garden was planned to the east, to be overlooked by the new Royal Apartments. At the same time the small physic garden created near the abbey became the origins of the Royal Botanic Garden, Edinburgh. In the early eighteenth century these gardens were still flourishing. Daniel Defoe described them in *A Tour Through the Whole Island of Great Britain* of 1724: 'one is like our apothecaries' garden at Chelsea, called a physic garden, and is tolerably well stored with simples, and some exotics of value; and, particularly, I was told, there was a rhubarb tree, or plant, and which throve very well.'

By the time Queen Victoria and her family stayed at the Palace, the gardens were overgrown and the lower end of the Royal Mile consisted of slums and industrial buildings. Prince Albert took a close interest in the redevelopment of the Palace's immediate surroundings. A new carriage approach was made to the north, avoiding the not very salubrious Canongate, but in the process the Privy Garden was swept away. New planting areas were created to the north and south of the Palace. To the east, the garden wall provided the same effect as an original eighteenth-century ha-ha, or hidden ditch, concealing the actual boundary of the garden and giving the impression that it flowed naturally into the park beyond. Screens of trees were planted to hide the nearby breweries and gasworks. During the reign of George V and Queen Mary the gardens continued to be improved, and were laid out with herbaceous borders and a long rockery.

Today the gardens are regularly improved and updated. New borders were created for the Silver and Golden Jubilees and new trees have been planted recently. The grounds come to life during the summer and provide the setting for The Queen's Garden Party, held annually in July for around 8,000 people.

LEFT
The Queen and Lord Airlie, Captain-General of the Royal Company of Archers, at a garden party in the Palace gardens in 2009.

BELOW
Looking across the gardens towards the remains of Holyrood Abbey.

THE ROYAL COMPANY OF ARCHERS

The Royal Company of Archers was founded in 1678 as an archery club. It was created The King's Bodyguard for Scotland by George IV on his visit in 1822. The Royal Company provides detachments for investitures and for the Garden Party at Holyroodhouse, and Guards of Honour for the installation of Knights of the Thistle, the opening of the Scottish Parliament and other ceremonial occasions attended by The Queen. Members carry a longbow and wear a distinctive uniform of dark green tunic and trousers, a Balmoral bonnet with the Royal Company's badge and an eagle feather. Archery remains an important aspect of the Royal Company's life and many members participate in the annual competitions, including The Queen's Prize, which takes place in the gardens of the Palace in June.

ABOVE LEFT
The Royal Company of Archers on duty at the annual Garden Party.

CENTRE LEFT
A member of the Royal Company of Archers takes aim in the gardens.

BELOW LEFT
The Queen is ceremonially presented by the Royal Company of Archers with a 'Reddendo'. This was originally a pair of barbed arrows resting on a green velvet cushion. Here The Queen is receiving a gold and enamel pen stand.